Air Fryer: Fish TOP 20 most popular recipes

By Olivia Mart

Air Fryer: Fish - TOP 20 most popular recipes

Recipes

Thank you for your choice!

Take your gift on the last page!

Copyright 2016 by MalMar Publishing - All rights reserved.

All rights Reserved. No part of this publication or the information in it may be quoted from or reproduced in any form by means such as printing, scanning, photocopying or otherwise without prior written permission of the copyright holder.

Disclaimer and Terms of Use: Effort has been made to ensure that the information in this book is accurate and complete, however, the author and the publisher do not warrant the accuracy of the information, text and graphics contained within the book due to the rapidly changing nature of science, research, known and unknown facts and internet. The Author and the publisher do not hold any responsibility for errors, omissions or contrary interpretation of the subject matter herein. This book is presented solely for motivational and informational purposes only.

Table of Contents

Introduction 5

   Baja Style Fish Tacos 6

   California Fish and "Chips" 8

   Crumbed Fish 10

   Lobster Ravioli...12

   Firecracker Salmon 14

   Fish & Chips...16

   Fish & Chips 2..18

   Fish Tacos..20

   Corn flake White Swai Fish 22

   Fried-Fish Sandwiches with Jalapeño-Spiked Tomatoes.......................23

   Garlic-Lemon Mackerel...25

   Herb And Garlic Fish 27

   Honey Garlic Salmon...29

   Honey-Glazed Salmon...31

   Parmesan Salmon 33

   Panko-Crusted Fish Sticks 35

   Fishcakes with beetroot and parsnip chips..................................37

   Sweet and Spicy Salmon 39

   Sea Bass with Spicy Soy Sauce Recipe..41

   Simple Salmon & Asparagus 43

Introduction

Welcome to the world of healthy eating! We are glad you have joined us!

Fish is on the menu today!!!

Bass, Salmon, Swai, Mackarel, Hailbut and many more – all of those can be made in an Air fryer within an hour! Easy and without a hustle. In half and hour you can enjoy perfectly cooked fish, yes, the one that falls apart with a touch of a fork. Avoiding problems like watching and peeking at your fish every 5 minutes, or trying to measure the perfect time to make it crunchy and not burn it under the broiler! All of those are in the past!

We have searched for the easiest recipes and adapted your favorite ones! Now you can enjoy new and improved fish recipes with no more, than a tablespoon of oil (comparing to the pan full of oil for deep frying? I see an obvious winner here!).

Flaky, juicy salmon; delicious fish tacos, seafood ravioli and many, many more choices are just waiting to be cooked! So, let's get cooking…!

Baja Style Fish Tacos

Servings: 6

Prep Time: 35min   Cook Time: 15min   Yield: 6 to 8 servings

Ingredients

1 cup flour
1 cup dark mexican beer
1/3 cup mayonnaise
2/3 cup sour cream
1 tsp grated lemon zest
2 tbsp fresh lemon juice
2 tbsp water
Salt, black pepper
Spray oil
1 cup flour
2 pounds skinned halibut cut into 5 by 1/2-inch strips
corn tortillas
shredded cabbage
cups salsa

Directions

In a bowl combine flour with salt and pepper. Mix in beer, let it sit for 15 min.

Cream Sauce:

Mix together sour cream and mayo. Stir in lemon zest, lemon juice and water. Salt and pepper, to taste.

Fish:

Preheat Air fryer to 180 degrees C.

Rub the fish strips with salt and pepper, cover with flour. After that, coat each strip in beer batter, you have prepared prior.

Spray fish with oil, lay out in the Air fryer and cook for 12 to 14 min.

Air Fryer: Fish - TOP 20 most popular recipes

Prepare tacos by laying each fish strip (or two!) on a tortilla; add shredded cabbage, salsa and sour cream.

Nutrition Facts

Serving Size: 1/6 of a recipe.

Amount Per Serving	% Daily Value
Calories: 323	16%
Calories from Fat: 130	19%
Total Fat: 14g	22%
Saturated Fat: 4g	20%
Cholesterol: 18mg	6%
Sodium: 1125mg	47%
Total Carbohydrates: 40g	13%
Fiber: 2g	8%
Sugars: 4g	
Protein: 2g	4%
Vitamin A:	3%
Vitamin C:	59%
Calcium:	5%
Iron:	10%

California Fish and "Chips"

Servings: 6

Prep Time: 1 hour Cook Time: 30min Yield: 6 servings

Ingredients

3 lbs white fish
Salt, black pepper
2 cups flour
½ cup milk mixed with ½ cup eggs
2 cups breadcrumbs

Guacamole:
1 cup ripe, avocado
1 tbsp lemon juice
2 tbsp fresh cilantro, chopped
2 tbsp diced tomatoes
1 tsp sriracha

"Chips" (French fries)
6 potatoes
½ gallon vegetable oil
Salt, black pepper

Directions

Preheat Airfryer to 180 degrees C.

Dry the fish off with paper towel, rub with salt and pepper. Coat with flour first, then eggs and milk, and last the breadcrumbs. Repeat with the rest of the fish.

Cook for 8 to 10 min.

Serve with "chips" and guacamole.

Guacamole:
Peel and cut avocado in half, get rid of the pit. Mash with a fork with some lemon juice. Mix in cilantro, sriracha and tomatoes.

Air Fryer: Fish - TOP 20 most popular recipes

Recipes

Chips:

Wash and peel the potatoes. Cut into long strips (like French fries). Rinse in cold water. Dry off potato slices. Preheat oil in the deep fryer. Blanch the fries for 3 min, then pull them out and let dry. Let sit in the fridge for about an hour, then deep fry in the preheated oil in smaller batches for about 4 min each. Lay out on the paper towels to catch extra oil. Season with salt.

Nutrition Facts

Serving Size: 1/6 of a recipe.

Amount Per Serving	% Daily Value
Calories: 5842	292%
Calories from Fat: 5150	773%
Total Fat: 618g	951%
Saturated Fat: 87g	435%
Cholesterol: 187mg	62%
Sodium: 833mg	35%
Total Carbohydrates: 65g	22%
Fiber: 3g	12%
Sugars: 9g	
Protein: 63g	115%
Vitamin A:	7%
Vitamin C:	66%
Calcium:	23%
Iron:	10%

Air Fryer: Fish - TOP 20 most popular recipes

Recipes

Crumbed Fish

Servings: 2

Prep Time: 10min   Cook Time: 12min   Yield: Serves: 2

Ingredients

4 tbsp vegetable oil
breadcrumbs
1 egg
4 fish fillets
1 lemon
Spices to taste

Directions

Preheat Airfryer to 180 degrees C.

Combine oil with breadcrumbs, until the mixture start falling apart easily.

Whisk the egg with spices.

Coat the fillets in egg then in breadcrumbs.

Cook in the Airfryer basket for 10 to 12 minutes, depending on the thickness of fillets.

Serve with lemon slices.

Nutrition Facts

Serving Size: 1/2 of a recipe.

Amount Per Serving	% Daily Value
Calories: 399	20%
Calories from Fat: 265	40%
Total Fat: 32g	49%
Saturated Fat: 5g	25%
Cholesterol: 182mg	61%
Sodium: 176mg	7%
Total Carbohydrates: 4g	1%

Air Fryer: Fish - TOP 20 most popular recipes

Recipes

Fiber: 0g	0%
Sugars: 0g	
Protein: 28g	51%
Vitamin A:	4%
Vitamin C:	24%
Calcium:	2%
Iron:	3%

Lobster Ravioli

Servings: 25

Prep Time: 30 min   Cook Time: 45 min

Ingredients

2 tbsp butter
1/2 cup minced carrots
1/2 cup minced celery
3/4 cup minced onion
thyme
1 minced garlic clove
3 oz water
2 lobsters (about 1.5 lbs each)
Grated Parmesan cheese
parsley
1 egg
salt, pepper, thyme, parsley
25 wonton wrappers

Directions

Boil the lobster in salted water for 15 min. When done place on the ice to cool off faster. Get all the meat from the tail and claws

Melt the butter in the pan on the stove top. Sauté carrots, celery and onion. Add in thyme and garlic. Fry for a minute, then add in water. Cover and cook until all the water is gone. Remove from the heat and let cool. Add in parsley, parmesan and cut up lobster meat. Salt and pepper, to taste.

Preheat Airfryer to 200 degrees.

Whisk egg with 2 tbsp of water, to prepare the egg wash. Lay out wonton wrappers and brush them with egg wash. Place a scoop of lobster mix and cover up with another wonton wrapper. Press down the edges to form ravioli. Repeat until lobster meat is gone. You can leave them as squares or reshape them into circles.

Lay Airfryer basket with baking paper and cook ravioli for 5-6 min.

Air Fryer: Fish - TOP 20 most popular recipes

Serve with marinara sauce!

Nutrition Facts

Serving Size: 1/25 of a recipe.

Amount Per Serving	% Daily Value
Calories: 57	3%
Calories from Fat: 26	4%
Total Fat: 3g	5%
Saturated Fat: 1g	5%
Cholesterol: 10mg	3%
Sodium: 88mg	4%
Total Carbohydrates: 6g	2%
Fiber: 0g	0%
Sugars: 1g	
Protein: 2g	4%
Vitamin A:	7%
Vitamin C:	0%
Calcium:	1%
Iron:	1%

Firecracker Salmon

Servings: 6

Cook Time: 30

Ingredients

- 6 salmon fillets
- 1/4 cup soy sauce
- 1/4 cup balsamic vinegar
- 1 tbsp honey
- 2 tbsp chopped garlic
- 2 tsp dried crushed red pepper
- 1 1/2 tsp ground ginger
- 1 tsp sesame oil
- 1/2 tsp table, salt
- 1/4 tsp onion powder

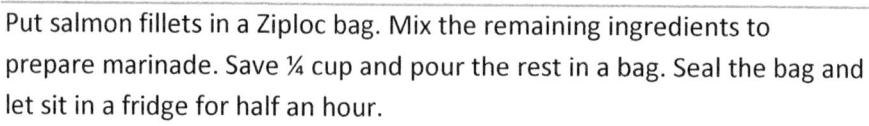

Directions

Put salmon fillets in a Ziploc bag. Mix the remaining ingredients to prepare marinade. Save ¼ cup and pour the rest in a bag. Seal the bag and let sit in a fridge for half an hour.

Preheat Air fryer to 200 degrees C.

Remove salmon from the fridge and out of the marinade. Cook in the Air fryer for 10 min, brushing the remaining marinade half way through the cooking. Remove the skin and once the fish is done it will flake easily.

Nutrition Facts

Serving Size: 1/6 of a recipe.

Amount Per Serving	% Daily Value
Calories: 189	9%
Calories from Fat: 167	25%
Total Fat: 19g	29%
Saturated Fat: 3g	15%
Cholesterol: 0mg	0%
Sodium: 559mg	23%
Total Carbohydrates: 5g	2%
Fiber: 0g	0%
Sugars: 4g	
Protein: 2g	4%
Vitamin A:	0%

Air Fryer: Fish - TOP 20 most popular recipes

Vitamin C:	0%
Calcium:	0%
Iron:	0%

Air Fryer: Fish - TOP 20 most popular recipes

Recipes

Fish & Chips

Servings: 2

Prep time: 30 min
Cook time: 25 min
Yield: 2

Ingredients

- 2 catfish fillets
- 1 egg
- breadcrumbs
- 1 25 gr package yellow tortilla chips
- 1 lemon (rind and juice)
- 1 tbsp parsley
- Salt, pepper

Chips:
- 4 potatoes
- Oil
- Salt, pepper

Directions

Cut up each fillet into 4 pieces and rub with lemon juice.
Crumble the chips and mix with breadcrumbs, parsley, lemon rind, salt and pepper. Remove to the plate.
Dip each fish piece in whisked egg, then in breadcrumb mix.
Cook in the Airfryer at 180 degrees C for 15 minutes.

Chips:

Wash and peel the potatoes. Cut them up into French fries slices.
Put them in the Airfryer basket and add some oil. Cook at 180 degrees C for 2 min. Shake well and cook for 8 more min. Shake again and cook for additional 15min.
Salt and pepper before serving.

Nutrition Facts

Serving Size: 1/2 of a recipe.

Amount Per Serving	% Daily Value
Calories: 209	10%

Air Fryer: Fish - TOP 20 most popular recipes

Calories from Fat: 35	5%
Total Fat: 4g	6%
Saturated Fat: 1g	5%
Cholesterol: 72mg	24%
Sodium: 373mg	16%
Total Carbohydrates: 37g	12%
Fiber: 3g	12%
Sugars: 4g	
Protein: 6g	11%
Vitamin A:	2%
Vitamin C:	24%
Calcium:	6%
Iron:	14%

Fish & Chips 2

Prep Time: :20   Cook Time: :10

Ingredients

- 2 tilapia fish fillets
- 2 tbsp lime juice
- 2 tbsp red chili flakes
- Salt, pepper
- 1 package tortilla chips
- 1 egg

Directions

Place the fillets in a Ziploc bag and pour in lime juice, chili flakes and salt/pepper. Marinate in the fridge for 20 min.

Crumble tortilla chips into small pieces, close to dust.

Preheat Airfryer to 320 degrees F.

Pull the fish out of the marinade and dip in the whisked egg and then in chips crumble.

Place fish in the Airfryer basket and cook for 10 minutes.

Nutrition Facts

Serving Size: 1 of a recipe.

Amount Per Serving	% Daily Value
Calories: 171	9%
Calories from Fat: 39	6%
Total Fat: 5g	8%
Saturated Fat: 1g	5%
Cholesterol: 253mg	84%
Sodium: 195mg	8%
Total Carbohydrates: 0g	0%
Fiber: 0g	0%
Sugars: 0g	
Protein: 30g	55%
Vitamin A:	6%
Vitamin C:	0%
Calcium:	1%

Air Fryer: Fish - TOP 20 most popular recipes

Recipes

Iron:	5%

Fish Tacos

Ingredients

corn tortilla
peach salsa
cilantro
fresh halibut
1 can beer
1 1/2 cups flour
1 tsp baking powder
2 tbsp oil
1 tsp salt
cholula sauce
avocado cream:
1 large avocado
3/4 cup buttermilk
1/2 lime

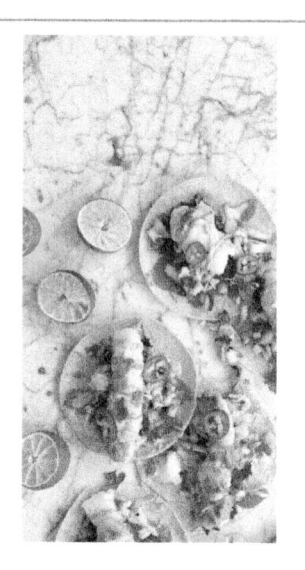

Directions

Slice halibut into strips. Coat with flour.

Combine flour, baking powder and salt. Add beer, a little bit at a time, to reach the consistency of pancake batter.

Dip strips into batter and lay them out on the well-greased Airfryer rack. Cook for 6 to 8 min at 200 degrees C.

Lay out tortillas; spread some peach salsa on each. Lay out the fish on top and spread some avocado sauce. Sprinkle with cilantro and Cholula.

Avocado cream:

Peel and cut up avocado. Mash it; add buttermilk and juice from lime. Mix well until smooth.

Nutrition Facts

Serving Size: 1 of a recipe.	Amount Per Serving	% Daily Value

Air Fryer: Fish - TOP 20 most popular recipes

Recipes

Calories: 1014	51%
Calories from Fat: 20	3%
Total Fat: 14g	22%
Saturated Fat: 1g	6%
Cholesterol: 8mg	3%
Sodium: 3165mg	132%
Total Carbohydrates: 175g	58%
Fiber: 6g	24%
Sugars: 8g	
Protein: 9g	16%
Vitamin A:	2%
Vitamin C:	40%
Calcium:	27%
Iron:	40%

Corn flake White Swai Fish

Ingredients

1 cup Corn flakes
4 White Swai fillets
Salt, pepper
Seasonings
1 tsp olive oil

Directions

Crumble Corn flakes to powder state. Add salt, pepper and any other seasonings you prefer best. Add oil and mix, until it starts to fall apart.

Press the fish down, so that the coating sticks, then flip and repeat.

Preheat Air fryer to 390 degrees F. Cook the fish for 12 min in a single layer.

Nutrition Facts

Serving Size: 1 of a recipe.

Amount Per Serving	% Daily Value
Calories: 905	45%
Calories from Fat: 27	4%
Total Fat: 4g	6%
Saturated Fat: 1g	5%
Cholesterol: 143mg	48%
Sodium: 4167mg	174%
Total Carbohydrates: 207g	69%
Fiber: 10g	38%
Sugars: 0g	
Protein: 14g	25%
Vitamin A:	4%
Vitamin C:	0%
Calcium:	1%
Iron:	13%

Fried-Fish Sandwiches with Jalapeño-Spiked Tomatoes

Servings: 4

Cook Time: 30 min   Yield: 4

Ingredients

flour
Salt, pepper
2 1/4 cups club soda
1 tsp ground cumin
1 tsp dried oregano
1 tsp hot paprika
6 haddock fillets
2 medium tomatoes
1 small yellow onion
1 jalapeño
1/4 cup chopped cilantro
4 kaiser rolls, cut in half and toasted
lettuce leaves

Directions

Combine flour and salt in a bowl. Mix in club soda until smooth. Place the bowl with batter on the ice bath and let chill for 10 min.

Rub salt, pepper, cumin, oregano and paprika into the fish.

Slice tomatoes, onion and jalapeno (seeded). Toss in a bowl with cilantro and salt.

Preheat Air fryer to 180 degrees C.

Coat each fillet in flour, then dip in the batter and cook for about 10 min, until golden brown on the outside.

Lay the lettuce leaves on each roll. Place fish on top, then tomato, onion and jalapeno slices. Close the sandwich with the other half of the roll and serve!

Nutrition Facts

Air Fryer: Fish - TOP 20 most popular recipes

Recipes

Serving Size: 1/4 of a recipe.

Amount Per Serving	% Daily Value
Calories: 23	1%
Calories from Fat: 0	0%
Total Fat: 0g	0%
Saturated Fat: 0g	0%
Cholesterol: 0mg	0%
Sodium: 39mg	2%
Total Carbohydrates: 4g	1%
Fiber: 1g	4%
Sugars: 0g	
Protein: 1g	2%
Vitamin A:	20%
Vitamin C:	25%
Calcium:	0%
Iron:	1%

Garlic-Lemon Mackerel

Ingredients

1 mackerel fillet
fresh red chili pepper
lemon juice
1 tbsp minced garlic
1 tbsp olive oil
salt

Directions

Clean the fillet and pat dry with paper towels.

Place the fish on top of the aluminum foil, skin side down.

Sprinkle with salt and lemon juice.

Spread out minced garlic and cut up chili pepper (don't forget to deseed it) evenly.

Spray with oil and place in the Air fryer.

Cook for 8 min at 180 degrees C.

Remove from the foil on to the plate and serve!

Nutrition Facts

Serving Size: 1 of a recipe.

Amount Per Serving	% Daily Value
Calories: 124	6%
Calories from Fat: 120	18%
Total Fat: 14g	22%
Saturated Fat: 2g	10%
Cholesterol: 0mg	0%
Sodium: 1mg	0%
Total Carbohydrates: 1g	0%
Fiber: 0g	0%
Sugars: 0g	
Protein: 2g	4%

Air Fryer: Fish - TOP 20 most popular recipes

Recipes

Vitamin A:	0%
Vitamin C:	0%
Calcium:	0%
Iron:	0%

Herb And Garlic Fish

Servings: 4

Prep Time: 10 mins   Cook Time: 30 mins   Yield: 4

Ingredients

300 gr seer fish
½ tsp salt
2 tbsp lemon juice
½ tsp turmeric powder
½ tsp red chili flakes
2 tsp mixed dried herbs
2 tsp garlic powder
½ tsp crushed black pepper
1 tsp garlic, paste
2 tbsp maida
1 tsp rice, flour
2 tsp corn flour
2 eggs
¼ tsp baking soda
1 cup bread crumbs
Spray oil

Directions

Cut up fish into stripes. Mix with lemon juice, turmeric, chili flakes, some mixed herbs, half of garlic powder, garlic paste, salt and pepper. Let sit for 10 min.

Combine maida, rice and corn flour and baking powder with eggs.

Put the fish in, so all the pieces are coated. Let sit for additional 10 min.

Add remaining herbs and garlic powder to the bread crumbs.

Cover the fish fingers with breadcrumbs and lay them out on the foil. Spray with oil.

Cook in the preheated to 180 degrees C Air fryer for 10 min, until slightly brown.

Serve with Tartar sauce.

Nutrition Facts

Serving Size: 1/4 of a recipe.

Amount Per Serving	% Daily Value
Calories: 13	1%
Calories from Fat: 7	1%
Total Fat: 1g	2%
Saturated Fat: 0g	0%
Cholesterol: 36mg	12%
Sodium: 11mg	0%
Total Carbohydrates: 0g	0%
Fiber: 0g	0%
Sugars: 0g	
Protein: 2g	4%
Vitamin A:	1%
Vitamin C:	0%
Calcium:	0%
Iron:	1%

Air Fryer: Fish - TOP 20 most popular recipes

Honey Garlic Salmon

Servings: 2

Prep Time: 10 min   Cook Time: 20 min   Yield: 2

Ingredients

- 1 lbs salmon fillet
- 1 tsp minced garlic
- 1/2 tsp minced ginger
- 4 tbsp honey
- 2 tbsp soy sauce

Directions

Mix honey, soy sauce, minced garlic and ginger in a bowl. Place the salmon in and marinate for 25-30 min.

Lineup Air fryer with foil, for easy clean up. Lay out salmon. Cook at 395 degrees F for 10 min. Brush with remaining marinade midway.

On the stove top bring the rest of the marinade to a boil to thicken it up.

Once the fish is done drizzle with thickened marinade and serve!

Nutrition Facts

Serving Size: 1/2 of a recipe.

Amount Per Serving	% Daily Value
Calories: 617	31%
Calories from Fat: 213	32%
Total Fat: 24g	37%
Saturated Fat: 4g	20%

Air Fryer: Fish - TOP 20 most popular recipes

Recipes

Cholesterol: 200mg	67%
Sodium: 689mg	29%
Total Carbohydrates: 36g	12%
Fiber: 0g	0%
Sugars: 34g	
Protein: 64g	116%
Vitamin A:	11%
Vitamin C:	0%
Calcium:	0%
Iron:	5%

Honey-Glazed Salmon

Ingredients

- 2 pcs salmon fillets
- 6 tbsp honey
- 6 tsp soy sauce
- 3 tsp rice wine
- 1 tsp water

Directions

Combine soy sauce, honey and wine in a bowl. Take some away and save it for dipping sauce.

Place salmon in the marinade and let it sit for 2 hours (or more if you have time).

Preheat Air fryer to 180 degrees C.

Cook salmon for 8 min, brushing with marinade midway, after flipping. Cook for 5 more minutes.

Heat remaining sauce on the stove top; let simmer for about a minute, until it thickens.

Serve salmon with thickened sauce.

Nutrition Facts

Serving Size: 1 of a recipe.

Amount Per Serving	% Daily Value
Calories: 30	2%
Calories from Fat: 0	0%
Total Fat: 0g	0%
Saturated Fat: 0g	0%
Cholesterol: 0mg	0%
Sodium: 1080mg	45%
Total Carbohydrates: 4g	1%
Fiber: 0g	0%

Air Fryer: Fish - TOP 20 most popular recipes

Recipes

Sugars: 4g	
Protein: 4g	7%
Vitamin A:	0%
Vitamin C:	0%
Calcium:	0%
Iron:	0%

Parmesan Salmon

Prep Time: 15   Cook Time: 30

Ingredients

- 4 salmon fillets
- Salt, pepper
- 2 tsp mayonnaise
- 2 tbsp grated parmesan
- ½ tsp sweet paprika

Directions

Run cold water over salmon and pat dry with paper towels. Salt and pepper, to taste.

Mix mayo and parmesan and brush over fillets. Sprinkle with extra parmesan and sweet paprika.

Line the Air fryer with foil and lay the salmon fillets out. Cook at 395 degrees F for 10 min.

To make the top of the fillets extra crispy you can set the fish in the oven and broil for a few min.

After that slide the fish off the foil, the skin should come off easily. Serve!

Nutrition Facts

Serving Size: 1 of a recipe.

Amount Per Serving	% Daily Value
Calories: 300	15%
Calories from Fat: 300	45%
Total Fat: 33g	51%
Saturated Fat: 5g	23%
Cholesterol: 15mg	5%

Air Fryer: Fish - TOP 20 most popular recipes   Recipes

Sodium: 270mg	11%
Total Carbohydrates: 0g	0%
Fiber: 0g	0%
Sugars: 0g	
Protein: 0g	0%
Vitamin A:	0%
Vitamin C:	0%
Calcium:	0%
Iron:	0%

Air Fryer: Fish - TOP 20 most popular recipes

Recipes

Panko-Crusted Fish Sticks

Ingredients

1 tbsp 2% milk
2 eggs
1 lbs halibut fillets
1 cup panko breadcrumbs
Salt, pepper
2 tbsp oil
1/4 cup sour cream
3 tbsp mayonnaise
2 tbsp bread-and-butter pickles
2 tsp minced capers

Directions

Cut up fillets into stripes (to make sticks).

Mix together milk and eggs. Nicely coat the fish in it.

In a Ziploc bag, combine bread crumbs with salt and pepper. Put the fish, seal and give it a gentle shake, to coat the fish sticks.

Preheat Air fryer to 180 degrees C.

Place the fish sticks in the Air fryer and spray with oil. Cook for 10 min, until nicely browned.

For dipping sauce:

Mix together sour cream, mayo, cut up pickles, capers, salt and pepper.

Serve the fish sticks with fresh made dipping sauce!

Nutrition Facts

Serving Size: 1 of a recipe.

Amount Per Serving	% Daily Value
Calories: 795	40%
Calories from Fat: 716	107%
Total Fat: 79g	122%

Air Fryer: Fish - TOP 20 most popular recipes

Recipes

Saturated Fat: 19g	94%
Cholesterol: 333mg	111%
Sodium: 3058mg	127%
Total Carbohydrates: 6g	2%
Fiber: 0g	0%
Sugars: 3g	
Protein: 11g	19%
Vitamin A:	13%
Vitamin C:	0%
Calcium:	9%
Iron:	5%

Fishcakes with beetroot and parsnip chips

Servings: 4

Ingredients

Mashed potatoes (from 3 potatoes)
zest and juice of 1 lemon
dill (chopped)
1 cup breadcrumbs
1 hot smoked trout (skinned, boned and flaked)
1 egg
Oil spray
Tartar sauce
Lemon slices

2 beetroots
1 parsnip
Spray oil

Directions

Boil and mash potatoes.

While mashed potatoes are cooling down, mix breadcrumbs with half of the dill and lemon zest.

Take a spoonful of trout and mix with a spoonful of potatoes, the rest of the dill and lemon juice. Form a patty.

Beat the egg. Dip the patties in the egg first, and then in breadcrumbs. Let the patties sit in a fridge for 30 min.

Preheat Air fryer to 180 degrees C.

Spray patties with oil and cook 4 at a time for 20 min, or until golden brown.

Beetroot and parsnip chips

Air Fryer: Fish - TOP 20 most popular recipes

Peel and slice beets and parsnip as thin as you can. Dry off with paper towels.

Preheat Air fryer to 200 degrees C.

Lightly spray with oil and cook a handful at a time for 10 min.

Let cool and sprinkle with salt.

Nutrition Facts

Serving Size: 1/4 of a recipe.

Amount Per Serving	% Daily Value
Calories: 357	18%
Calories from Fat: 63	9%
Total Fat: 7g	11%
Saturated Fat: 2g	10%
Cholesterol: 76mg	25%
Sodium: 400mg	17%
Total Carbohydrates: 51g	17%
Fiber: 4g	16%
Sugars: 5g	
Protein: 21g	38%
Vitamin A:	4%
Vitamin C:	26%
Calcium:	10%
Iron:	17%

Sweet and Spicy Salmon

Ingredients

salmon fillets

Marinade:
1 orange (juice and zest)
¼ cup honey
¼ cup soy sauce
1 tsp oil

Directions

Combine the ingredients for marinade. Reserve some for glazing later and pour the rest in a Ziploc bag. Put in the fish and let it sit for at least 20 min.

Lay out the Air fryer basket with foil to prevent sticking. Place the fish on the foil and spray with oil.

Cook for 10 min at 180 degrees C. Brush salmon with saved marinade about half way through.

Serve!

Nutrition Facts

Serving Size: 1 of a recipe.

Amount Per Serving	% Daily Value
Calories: 4	0%
Calories from Fat: 0	0%
Total Fat: 0g	0%
Saturated Fat: 0g	0%
Cholesterol: 0mg	0%
Sodium: 1mg	0%

Air Fryer: Fish - TOP 20 most popular recipes

Recipes

Total Carbohydrates: 1g	0%
Fiber: 0g	0%
Sugars: 0g	
Protein: 2g	4%
Vitamin A:	0%
Vitamin C:	0%
Calcium:	0%
Iron:	0%

Sea Bass with Spicy Soy Sauce Recipe

Ingredients

1 medium sea bass
Ginger slices
½ onion
1 pandan leaf
2 tsp corn flour
2 tbsp oil
Salt, pepper
Sauce:
2 tbsp soy sauce
2 dried chili
1 tbsp brown sugar
1 tsp oyster sauce
2 tbsp oil
½ onion
½ cup water
Pepper
Onion stalk

Directions

Clean the fish out, wash and dry well. Rub with salt, pepper and flour.

Stuff the bass with ginger and onion slices, add a pandan leaf. Spray both sides of the fish with oil.

Place the whole fish in the Air fryer basket. Cook for 20 at 230 degrees C. After 12 min, flip the fish. If you want the fish to get crispy, add 5 more min to the cooking time.

Spicy soy sauce:

On the stove top heat up the oil, sauté cut up onion with chili until transparent. Stir in soy sauce oyster sauce, sugar and water. Pull out the chili. Add cut up spring onion. Season, to taste. Simmer to thicken t sauce.

Drizzle over the cooked fish and serve!

Air Fryer: Fish - TOP 20 most popular recipes

Recipes

Nutrition Facts

Serving Size: 1 of a recipe.

Amount Per Serving	% Daily Value
Calories: 38	2%
Calories from Fat: 0	0%
Total Fat: 0g	0%
Saturated Fat: 0g	0%
Cholesterol: 0mg	0%
Sodium: 158mg	7%
Total Carbohydrates: 9g	3%
Fiber: 2g	7%
Sugars: 0g	
Protein: 1g	2%
Vitamin A:	0%
Vitamin C:	20%
Calcium:	0%
Iron:	1%

Simple Salmon & Asparagus

Servings: 4

Prep Time: 6 mins		Cook Time: 14 mins		Yield: 4

Ingredients

1 tsp chili powder
½ tsp salt
¼ tsp red pepper flakes
⅛ tsp onion powder
⅛ tsp garlic powder
⅛ tsp turmeric
1 lbs asparagus
garlic salt
4 salmon fillets
lemon juice

Directions

Combine all of the spices in a bowl.

Lay the salmon and asparagus on the foil and season (don't forget to save some seasonings for asparagus!).

Cook in the Air fryer for 10 min at 395 degrees F.

Repeat for the asparagus and cook for 5 min at 200 degrees C.

Drizzle lemon juice on the salmon and serve!

Nutrition Facts

Serving Size: 1/4 of a recipe.

Amount Per Serving	% Daily Value
Calories: 10	1%
Calories from Fat: 0	0%
Total Fat: 0g	0%
Saturated Fat: 0g	0%
Cholesterol: 0mg	0%
Sodium: 330mg	14%
Total Carbohydrates: 2g	1%
Fiber: 0g	0%
Sugars: 0g	
Protein: 0g	0%

Air Fryer: Fish - TOP 20 most popular recipes

Recipes

Vitamin A:	6%
Vitamin C:	0%
Calcium:	0%
Iron:	0%

Description

Get a delicious healthy dinner on the table in less than 20 minutes with this Simple Salmon & Asparagus. Total Time: 20 mins

Instant Pot Cooker Cookbook: 50 fast and clear recipes of delicious meals for people with any level of cooking skills *by Olivia Mart*

This book is only for those who are looking for instant pot recipes not only for everyday usage, but also for special occasions! Want to impress your friends and family with a shrimp risotto? Or maybe you'd like to delight true meat lovers with an ideal Beef Stroganoff? If your answer is yes but still you don't want to spend the whole day in front of the oven, then instant pot pressure cooker is a perfect solution for you and the only thing required is an ideal cookbook with all the useful recipes you need.

Search on Amazon

50 Best easy air fryer recipes by Olivia Mart **(NEW!)**

Have you recently purchased a brand new kitchen appliance such as, oh, I don't know, maybe an Air fryer? Is it still collecting dust on the shelf?

Well, it's time to unpack it, because you are about to become a chef in your own kitchen.

Search on Amazon

Air Fryer: Chicken: TOP 25 most popular recipes by Olivia Mart **(NEW!)**

For true chicken meat lovers ONLY!
25 most popular recipes based on fresh&juicy chicken meat for your air fryer.

This book contains detailed information on each of a recipe, including: list of required ingredients, time required for cooking, number of servings, nutrition facts and a commentary.

You can find there a number of delicious meals to your taste: sweet or spicy, crispy or juicy, but all of them are undoubtedly tasty.

Search on Amazon

Bonus

Take your gift!
http://books.marokso.com/

This book is about brain training and will be also useful to you

Index

B
Baja Style Fish Tacos 6

C
California Fish and Chips 8
Crumbed Fish 10

D
Deep Fried Lobster Ravioli 12

F
Firecracker Grilled Salmon 14
Fish & Chips 16
Fish & Chips 2 18
Fish Tacos 20
Fried Zucchini Batter 22
Fried-Fish Sandwiches with
 Jalapeño-Spiked Tomatoes .. 23

G
Garlic-Lemon Mackerel (Saba Fish) 25

H
Herb And Garlic Fish 27
Honey Garlic Salmon 29
Honey-Glazed Salmon 31

O
Oven Roasted Salmon with
 Parmesan 33

P
Panko-Crusted Fish Sticks 35

R
Rustic fishcakes with beetroot
 and parsnip chips 37

S
Salmon Fish 39
Sea Bass with Spicy Dark Soy
 Sauce Recipe 41
Simple Salmon & Asparagus 43

Printed in Great Britain
by Amazon